Old KELTY

by
Guthrie Hutton

D1579262

Contractors' carts like this one were the precursors of the large trucks that carry the name of Kelty around the country today.

© Guthrie Hutton 2005
First published in the United Kingdom, 2005,
by Stenlake Publishing Ltd.
Telephone: 01290 551122
Printed by Cordfall Ltd., Glasgow, G21 2QA

ISBN 1 84033 336 7

**The publishers regret that they cannot supply
copies of any pictures featured in this book.**

ACKNOWLEDGEMENTS

In researching the history of the mining industry I have talked to a number of Kelty folk who all contributed to the base of knowledge used in compiling this little book. Although not directly involved, I must thank them for their help. Specifically I must thank Jim Douglas, artist, poet and all round good guy whose help in providing pictures and local knowledge has been immense. Cathy's cups of tea were always welcome too. I must also thank Bill Fiet who helped with additional pictures, as did the splendid Scottish Mining Museum at Newtongrange and Robert Grieves of Paisley. The excellent local history facility at Dunfermline Library was very useful and the staff there and at other Fife libraries were also most helpful. I should also pay tribute to the impressive work of the Kelty Heritage Group who have done much to keep the story of their village alive.

FURTHER READING

The books listed below were used by the author during his research. None of them are available from Stenlake Publishing. Those interested in finding out more are advised to contact their local bookshop or reference library.

Arnot, R. Page, *A History of the Scottish Miners*, 1955
Brotchie, Alan W., *The Dunfermline and District Tramways Company*, 1978
Bruce, William Scott, *The Railways of Fife*, 1980
Gibson, Revd Ivor, *The Spirit of Lassodie*, 2003
Gifford, John, *The Buildings of Scotland, Fife*, 1988
Haynes, Nick, *Perth & Kinross, An Illustrated Architectural Guide*, 2000
Kelty Community Council, Kelty Calendar, various years
Kelty Heritage Group, *Welcome to the Independent Republic of Kelty*, 1999
Kelty Heritage Group, *Kelty Images*, 2004
Muir, Augustus, *The Fife Coal Company Limited*, 1947
North British Railway Study Group Journal, No. 59, June 1995
Silver, Owen, *The Roads of Fife*, 1987

This evocative view from the 1930s captures the very essence of Kelty – a community nestling in pleasant countryside, but dominated by that hardest of all hard industries, coal mining.

INTRODUCTION

Through the early nineteenth century a number of hamlets including Oakfield, Kelty, Grievesland and Bridgend were strung out along the Great North Road. Many of their inhabitants earned a living by digging coal. The workings were relatively small-scale and did little more than nibble at the tip of deeper riches, but demand for coal was growing and the industry was seeking new areas to exploit. Railways were expanding and by the 1860s had made it possible to move heavy loads to and from almost anywhere. The small rural communities of West Fife were about to reap a whirlwind of economic, social and environmental change.

One agent of that change was the Fife Coal Company. Formed in 1872, it took over the existing workings of Kelty Colliery and with it the mineral rights, which it began to exploit in 1874 by sinking a new pit. By the scale of what had gone before it was huge, and it needed people to develop and work it: quite suddenly there was a new village on the map and it took the colliery name, Kelty.

The company was not content to stop there and within twenty years was sinking another, bigger colliery. As a result Kelty's population grew from a few hundred people to over 8,000, and despite having more residents than many historic burghs it remained a village with no burghal status and no town council. It was a situation which gave the Fife Coal Company a lot of power, for although it didn't own the village, it had enormous influence over its affairs.

Thus totally dependent on the coal industry and one major employer, Kelty thrived and for a time prospered, but after the First World War there was less money and more industrial unrest in an increasingly troubled industry. Nationalisation in 1947 brought renewed hope, but for Kelty it was short-lived, with all the local pits

closing down in the 1960s. Men had to travel further to find work and families began to move out.

The demise of the industry left the village with a legacy of abandoned pits and property. Similar decay was spread right across West Fife, and in 1966 Fife Council launched one of the biggest and most imaginative reclamation schemes in the country, culminating in the creation of Lochore Meadows Country Park. Thus there is now little trace of the industry that created Kelty, but far from disappearing the village is finding a new purpose, helped by the modern equivalent of the Great North Road, the M90, which has placed Kelty within easy commuting distance of Edinburgh.

Ironically the new road's construction caused excitement when it cut through seams of coal and a form of coal winning returned briefly with opencast operations. Sacks of coal, carried through the village by competitors in a gala day race, have also kept a link with the past, but it is deep mining that is embedded in the soul. Memorials to miners have been erected outside the library and where the Lindsay Colliery once stood. Time moves on, but Kelty's origins won't be forgotten quickly.

Kelty Cross in the 1950s.

In the eighteenth century Scotland's roads were often little better than packhorse tracks, but the Great North Road, from Queensferry to Perth and beyond, was an exception. It crossed a bridge over the Lochfitty Burn, seen in the picture on the left, at the hamlet of Cantsdam. The bridge is thought to have been built in the seventeenth century, was repaired in 1722 and rebuilt in the 1940s. The name Cantsdam suggests that the burn was harnessed at one time, possibly to drive the local mill, create a ford, or drive machinery for a mine. Mining was a principal occupation for the hamlet's residents, who worked at outcropping coal seams. Cantsdam was also where Beath Parish School was located in the days prior to the provision of universal education, when fewer than 1,000 people lived in the parish. On the left of the upper picture is the Glen Tavern, which at the start of the twentieth century claimed to provide 'quality unequalled' and 'the best beer in the district'.

We take roads almost for granted these days, and when their standard of repair falls below acceptable levels we roundly condemn councils, contractors and governments, but in the eighteenth century it would have been difficult to know who to curse because no one was really in charge. An attempt to improve the country's roads came with the Turnpike Acts, which allowed investors to take over sections of road, improve them and charge tolls for their use. The word turnpike comes from the barrier that was used to stop the traffic. It had spikes which were laid flat when the barrier was turned to clear the road for those who had paid their dues. The Great North Road became a turnpike road in the 1750s, making it one of the earliest in Scotland. Its original line is seen here at Oakfield in the early twentieth century, and can still be seen today, although few of the buildings in the picture have survived.

LOWER OAKFIELD, KELTY

Turnpike trusts had the power to alter the line of the roads they administered, but first had to obtain permission from Parliament. The Great North Road trustees applied for such approval in 1809. Originally the road ran in a straight line from Cantsdam to the Kelty Burn, but in doing so went up and over a number of hills, some of which were very steep for horse-hauled traffic. The new route was not straight, but lay on flatter ground to the east of the original road. It effectively bypassed all the little hamlets, which created a problem for the Dunfermline & District Tramways Co. when it extended its track from Cowdenbeath. This ran beside the new Great North Road towards Kelty, but to get into the village it had to cut across country between the new and old roads just south of Oakfield. This section of track, known as the 'car cutting', emerged on to the old road just behind where the children are gathered in this picture looking towards Cantsdam.

The trams operated on a single track system with passing places, one of which is seen on the facing page, and terminated just past the Kelty crossroads in front of the Gothenburg Hall. The service, which ran between Kelty and Cowdenbeath, began in 1910 and reached its peak of passenger numbers in 1922. At the fountain in Cowdenbeath the Kelty trams linked up with others going to and from Dunfermline. Tramcars rapidly became part of everyday street life as is evident in this view of Oakfield Street looking towards the cross. On the left is a milk cart – or perhaps a 'soor-dook cairt' – one that travelled around selling buttermilk, ideal for that bowl of morning porridge! The heap at the side of the road on the right is probably a delivery of coal. It was common practice for coal to be dumped like this and for the householder to have to barrow or carry it in buckets to their own bunker, where it was carefully stowed with rakers (big lumps) to the back and churls (small pieces) to the front.

The popularity of the trams fell away as buses started to offer more direct services to Dunfermline. Without the constraint of rails they could also travel to far-off places like Kirkcaldy, which appears to be the destination of this Italian-built Lancia of A. & A. Young. The company started operating in 1922, the year the trams peaked, and was one of a number of operators competing for the Kelty custom in the 1920s. It was all too much for the trams, which ceased running in 1931, but while they were failing A. & A. Young thrived, buying up or amalgamating with the competition. By 1931 it had a near monopoly of local services, but then it too was taken over by Walter Alexander & Sons which established a garage at Oakfield. From there services radiated across Fife and east central Scotland with, on board, one of the most enduring group of characters in Fife's, if not Scotland's, folklore – the conductresses known as Kelty Clippies. Their fame for giving quick-fire backchat and taking no nonsense terrified some passengers, amused others and inspired poets and artists to create a lasting memory of them.

Two of the four corners of Kelty crossroads, seen in this view looking north, were occupied by pubs operated by the Kelty Public House Society Limited. This was set up following the passing in 1893 of the Industrial & Providential Societies Act, which provided for licensed premises to be opened as co-operative ventures to finance civic improvements. The idea was pioneered in Sweden, so the pubs were known as Gothenburgs, or 'Goths'. Those at the cross were No. 1 Goth (to the right) and No. 2 Goth (left). Kelty Public House Society eventually built four of these establishments, although No. 4 Goth was never used as a pub. Employers like the Fife Coal Company welcomed the Goths as a way of controlling the sale of liquor to the workforce, and the company threw its weight behind proposals to set up a public house society in the village. Although there was a strong anti-drink element to the idea, local temperance groups opposed the first license application, but with backing from such a powerful patron it was bound to succeed.

Goths differed from other pubs in a number of ways. Management was 'disinterested' as whoever was in charge received a salary and had no stake in the profits. Interiors were Spartan, without frills, and there were no games like darts and dominoes – the whole concept was geared to maximising the amount of money available to spend on good causes. The Kelty society funded a district nurse and gave grants to Dunfermline & District Hospital, the Aitken Baths, Moray Institute, the brass and pipe bands and various other clubs and societies. It also erected this large hall, which was opened in September 1910 and added a real sense of scale to Main Street. The way the coal industry developed rapidly over a short space of time in the east of Scotland gave the companies involved the power to influence what happened in villages in a way that did not happen elsewhere, so while many of these co-operative pubs were set up in Fife and Midlothian there were very few elsewhere. The civic function of the Goths may also have attracted the big companies, because the money raised could be used to pay for things that they might otherwise have had to fund.

One of the highlights in the annual village calendar, the Children's Gala Day, also received funds from the Public House Society. In this undated picture the gala parade is seen passing the cross with the Gothenburg Hall in the background, enhanced by a clock tower which was added in 1926. The hall was used for a wide variety of social activities including musical entertainments which had been a main beneficiary of the society's funding from the outset. It was also used to show films in the years before the Regal Cinema, built a little further up the street in 1939, provided competition. In common with most places of public entertainment across the country, the hall declined after the 1950s, being used for a time as a bingo hall and then a garment factory before being demolished in the 1970s. The Regal Cinema was also demolished in the 1990s, and its site is now occupied by Fife Council's local office which, like the old Goth Hall, displays a prominent clock.

The picture of the Gothenburg Hall on page 10 shows, beyond it, a small two-storey block with shops on the ground floor. Painted on the gable wall is a sign advertising it as Forrests Warehouse, a shop operated by John Forrest of Cowdenbeath that offered tailoring and clothing at the 'keenest prices'. That sign, although much weathered and partly obscured by the single-storey shop now occupied by Oak Hygiene, is still visible, but Forrests is long gone. It had clearly been split into smaller units when this picture showing hardware, sweetie and newsagent's shops was taken. These have changed owners and functions over the years and are now occupied by a small supermarket, taxi office and barber's shop. The adjoining block, to the north, was used by Dick's Co-operative Institutions, a privately operated rival to the Kelty Co-operative Society. The original three-storey building was reduced to two following a fire on the upper floor.

Main Street was Kelty's principal shopping street, as is evident in this view looking back down the brae towards the cross. The picture is difficult to date precisely, but there are clues. It is clearly after 1926, when the Gothenburg Hall's tower was added, and there appear to be no tram tracks, dating it to after 1931 but before the construction of the Regal Cinema in 1939. As with the shops on the facing page, all has now changed, with a bakery chain, pharmacy and unisex hair stylists (a concept unthinkable in mining's heyday) having replaced such standards of the Scottish high street as the Buttercup Dairy. The Kelty shop was one of over 250 operated by the Leith-based company that prided itself in the spotless cleanliness of its premises, and in observing the mantra that 'Even though a wrong is as black as Egypt's night, the customer is always right'. Just out of view on the left was the village's first police station, where presumably the view of the customer tended to differ from that of the Buttercup Dairy.

The roads forming Kelty's crossroads are remarkable in their geometry, both straight as arrows and meeting at a right angle to form a perfect cross. This view, looking west up Cocklaw Street in the late 1940s, was used as a picture postcard and sent to Devon by someone on holiday in Kelty in January 1950. The village might seem an unlikely winter retreat for people from the south-west of England, and indeed Scotland's tourist authorities should be wary of adopting such an idea because, as this extract from the message home shows, the main attraction is no longer there: 'We had a wonderful trip down one of the coal mines here – 630 feet below the surface then about two miles to the actual coal face. My word what awful conditions these miners have to work under, I would not have one of their jobs for £10 a day.' The comparison with today's monetary values is almost as interesting as the comment about mining conditions.

Few of the buildings in this picture of Cocklaw Street have survived, although one that has, in the left foreground, is another of Kelty's licensed premises, the Oakfield Hotel. This end of the street, close to the cross, was where the Kelty Co-operative Society had most of its stores – and 'the store' is what people in Kelty, as elsewhere, called their local co-op. Scotland has a proud place in the co-operative movement with a number of small friendly and victualling societies predating the establishment in 1832 of the Rochdale Friendly Co-operative Society (regarded as the movement's pioneer). The peak of registrations in Scotland was in the 1860s. Kelty followed in the 1870s, reflecting the period when the village began to expand so rapidly. The shop with the prominent pediment on the right was the central grocery and, closer to the camera, the awnings are shielding the butcher's shop window and that of the branch where household goods and ironmongery were sold. The society also had retail outlets for bread, milk, clothing and footwear, offered services like plumbing, joinery and funerals, and had branches in other parts of the village.

At the start of the nineteenth century Beath Parish had one church, south of Cantsdam, at Kirkton. It was old, cold and damp, but it held 250 people and when the weather was good it was well-attended. The expansion of the coal industry brought a greatly increased number of worshipers, which in Kelty amounted to congregations representing three separate Protestant traditions by the end of the nineteenth century. They each needed a new church and all three were built at the same time. This picture shows the Church of Scotland, which was erected in the centre of the village on the corner of Oakfield Street and Station Road in 1894–96. Regarded as the Established Church, it was also known as Oakfield Church and was designed by architect John Houston with accommodation for 500 worshippers. There was no Catholic church in the village until 1922 when St Joseph's was opened off Cocklaw Street, but then few Catholics lived in this part of the country until the mining industry drew them to the village, mainly from the old pits of Lanarkshire.

Oakfield Church, on the left of this early twentieth century view, is the only one of the three Protestant churches erected in the 1890s still in use as a church following the amalgamation of the congregations in 1974. The church hall, which post-dates this picture, was added in 1932/33. It still exists, as do the buildings on the right, and indeed Station Road is one of the few streets in Kelty which remains much the same today as it did when many of these old pictures were taken. The most obvious difference is the state of the road and footpaths – before these were properly formed their surfaces alternated between mud and stoor depending on the season or the weather. Another change is the name, which was originally South Black Road. At the foot of Station Road, modern housing has taken the place of the old miners' rows known as Nasmyth Place. They were conveniently sited for the Lindsay Colliery, which is now marked at the road end by a memorial, erected in 1996, to the nine men who died in the explosion at the pit in 1957.

One of the first amenities funded by the Kelty Public House Society was the bowling green, which was laid out on the site of an old colliery formerly owned by the Earl of Moray, the principal landowner in the area. The ground sloped, so it had to be filled and levelled before being surfaced with turf brought all the way from Irvine in Ayrshire. The formal opening took place in July 1902. Five years later the club joined the Scottish Bowling Association and since then its members have enjoyed many competitive successes. Although the Kelty Public House Society met the initial costs of setting up the green, clubhouse and flagpole, the bowlers had to pay an annual fee back to the society. This continued until the latter was wound up in the early 1960s, at which point Kelty Bowling Club took responsibility for the facility. They put down a marker for the future in 1983 by extending the clubhouse. Beyond the green here is Station Road, with the war memorial on the left.

The Kelty Public House Society also provided funds for the village's war memorial which was unveiled by Sir Charles Adam in June 1921. A crowd of 5,000 people watched the ceremony. The memorial is a very fine tribute to the men who gave their lives in war and was created by the Edinburgh-based sculptor William Birnie Rhind, whose father and brother were also architectural sculptors. At the start of both world wars of the twentieth century, Kelty men, in common with miners elsewhere, were quick to volunteer for the forces. Only later, as the conflicts dragged on, did governments realise that winning coal was essential to winning wars and introduced measures to ensure production levels. Men were brought back from the front and mining was made a reserved occupation to stop others leaving the industry. During the Second World War, men who became known as Bevin Boys were conscripted into the pits in a controversial scheme devised by Ernest Bevin, the Minister of Fuel and Power.

War Memorial, Station Road, Kelty

The station was a long way from the end of Station Road, but if the railway was inconvenient for passengers it was well-placed for the collieries. As well as the main line between Edinburgh and Perth, a lot of other tracks converged on Kelty. In the left foreground is the West Fife Mineral Railway which ran up from Townhill, past the Lindsay Pit. Beyond the footbridge the tracks can be seen branching off in the direction of Kelty No. 3 Pit and Blairenbathie Colliery. The trucks on the right could be going in or out of the Aitken Colliery, or along the Lochore Branch to the Mary Pit. To the south of Kelty Station was another junction where the Lumphinnans and Kelty Branch line served Lumphinnans No. XI, otherwise known as the Peesweep Pit. Indeed, so many tracks radiated from Kelty that when a locomotive's axle broke just south of the Lumphinnans junction in September 1906 the carriages were able to be hauled back and re-routed via Cowdenbeath, and although the broken engine still blocked the main line disruption to other services was minimal. It is hard to believe that a railway hub once occupied today's trackless landscape.

The Fife Coal Company was established in 1872 with the takeover of the Beath & Blairadam Colliery Company, which operated a number of pits in and around Kelty. One of these was the Kelty Colliery where three shafts had already been sunk. The new company, however, was not content just to work these old pits and began sinking two new shafts on a site adjacent to the West Fife Mineral Railway. Initially known as Kelty Nos 4 and 5, the new shafts were effectively a new colliery which became known as the Lindsay Colliery after the first chairman of the company, William Lindsay. They were taken down 71 fathoms (the fathom, six feet, was commonly used in the mining industry as a unit of measure) to the Lochgelly Splint seam and the new pit began to wind coal when that was reached. Not content with that, however, the company carried on sinking No. 4 shaft to the Dunfermline Splint coal at 130 fathoms. No. 5 shaft was left at its original depth and became known as the 'wee pit'. The colliery, which remained in production until 1965, was referred to as the 'Grand Old Lady'.

Soon after the Lindsay sinking began, the company appointed a 23-year-old mining engineer, Charles Carlow, as its manager – a big job for a young man, but people backed youthful talent in those days. He made an instant impact, mechanising old workings or ruthlessly closing them down when output did not match the company's need for quality. He also disagreed with the siting of the Lindsay pits, but the decision on where Kelty's next major sinking was to be was his. Charles Carlow drove a 550-fathom underground mine from the Lindsay and in March 1893 began sinking a new shaft to meet it. Three years later cages were running to the Lochgelly Splint coal while sinking continued to the deeper Dunfermline Splint at 212 fathoms. The new pit was named the Aitken Colliery after Thomas Aitken of Nivingston who had succeeded William Lindsay as chairman. Initially there was only one brick-topped, timber-lined shaft, which would have been illegal but for the connecting mine to the Lindsay Pit. This provided an alternative means of escape if the shaft became unusable for any reason, which it did in 1897 when a fire broke out on the surface. A second shaft was sunk to 95 fathoms after the First World War.

Underground the Aitken became a jewel in the Fife Coal Company's crown, turning out a consistent level of production year after year and also setting output records. These production levels were achieved from seams that dipped and rose like the braes along Kelty High Street, sometimes with gradients of 1 in 2, which made the consistency all the more remarkable. The company sited a power station at the Aitken to supply most of its pits with electricity, and in the 1940s, after the coal industry came under state control, two concrete cooling towers were added. Nationalisation of the industry in 1947 gave Kelty's miners reason to feel optimistic about the future. Their pits, and Aitken in particular, were highly regarded and their village was being transformed by new council housing spreading across Kelty Hill. Despite this the good times came to a shuddering halt in the early to mid-1960s when, as suddenly as it had all started, industrial-scale deep mining in West Fife ceased. Aitken Colliery closed in 1963.

One of the early pits taken over by the Fife Coal Company was at Blairenbathie, but its coal was poor-quality, and fearful that this would give the company a bad name, Charles Carlow closed it. He had the machinery transferred to a new sinking at Leven and also moved the company's head office from Kelty to there. That was in the 1870s, but the industry hadn't given up on Blairenbathie and a new pit sinking was begun in 1895. The newly formed Fife & Kinross Coal Company took it over two years later, and in 1901 that company was absorbed by the Fife Coal Company. Faults and intrusions made it a difficult and ultimately unprofitable pit to work, leading to its closure during the industrial troubles of the 1920s. In the mid-1940s the Fife Coal Company opened a number of small drift mines to shallower levels and one of these, sited to the east of the old colliery, was known as Blairenbathie. It was taken over by the National Coal Board in 1947 and worked until 1962.

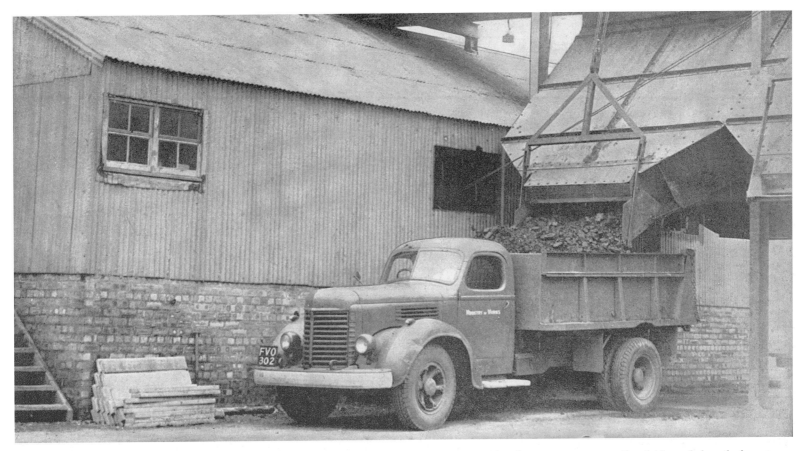

Blairenbathie was one of several drift mines opened by the Fife Coal Company in the 1940s. The idea was to extract coal quickly and cheaply from areas where reserves were known to exist, but not in quantities that justified a major sinking. It was based on American mining practice where the philosophy was to 'take the railway down the mine', although in fact the rails that went into the mines were for mine cars and not railway trucks. The first of these developments was Benarty Mine to the north-east of Kelty, from where coal was taken to the Aitken Colliery washery by lorries like the one seen here. The Ministry of Works name on its door suggests the picture dates from around the time of the industry's nationalisation in 1947. When it took over, the National Coal Board found it had a problem: new pits would take ten or more years to develop while many old, exhausted ones had to be closed. To fill the gap and maintain coal supplies it opened a number of small drift mines based on those developed around Kelty by the Fife Coal Company. These were never intended to last for long and most closed quite quickly (Benarty, for instance, in 1959) but a couple – Sorn in Ayrshire and Roger in Upper Nithsdale – lasted into the 1980s.

The mining industry created Lassodie, to the west of Kelty, and when it had finished with it destroyed it. In many respects it was not one village but a series that grew with different pit developments. In the 70 or so years of its existence there were up to eleven sinkings, mainly by Thomas Spowart & Co. Lassodie had all the trappings of a village: a pub, church, school (opened in 1877) and a local co-operative society, which was eventually taken over by the one from Kelty. It had a thriving football team which played in an all-black strip and gained a fearsome reputation for excessively robust play. The last pit closed in 1931 and the village was progressively cleared in compliance with conditions imposed when mining began. Opencast workings have since removed other surviving traces, and the only tangible evidence of this lost village is the war memorial relocated to beside the B912 Kelty to Kingseat road.

Facing page: The sign in the background identifies this group as the Kelty Soup Kitchen but doesn't, alas, say which year it dates from. It is thought to be 1912, although the men and women's clothing could equally date it to 1894, and presumably the clothes are not what folk wore when stirring the soup pots but a post-strike reflection of pride in what they did – even the dog looks pleased. Scotland's small pit-based mining unions took a long time to come together and form so-called 'county' unions, although the first of these was in Fife. A Scottish federation of county unions was agreed in 1894 and in the same year joined the Miners' Federation of Great Britain (MFGB) at a time when owners were trying to implement substantial cuts in wages. This sparked the 1894 strike which lasted for fifteen weeks in the rest of Scotland and seventeen in Fife, reflecting a failure to act together which weakened the union position. In 1912, however, when negotiations over the MFGB's demand for a fair minimum wage broke down, the first ever national miners' strike was called. It lasted for six weeks and although it achieved few concrete gains, the impact on the industry of the miners acting together for the first time was immense.

Miners' housing was often very poor and the standard of provision made by the coal companies varied widely. The Fife Coal Company was neither the best nor the worst in this regard, and an appropriate assessment of its performance would perhaps have been an average 'could have done better'. The houses in the pictures on this page were intended for tradesmen and officials such as oversmen, engineers and electricians, and were of a significantly higher standard than ordinary miners' accommodation. Moray Villas, the four homes in this picture, were built in 1919 with a living room, kitchen, scullery, bathroom, toilet and space for coal storage on the ground floor, and three bedrooms upstairs.

This picture shows some of the twenty Shiels Cottages built close to Moray Villas in 1924/25. They had three rooms plus a kitchen, bathroom, toilet, scullery with washing tubs and coal cellar. The emphasis in both of these developments was towards better sanitary arrangements than the communal outdoor wash houses and dry toilets of earlier miners' rows.

Although powers to provide housing were given to local authorities in 1909, the demand had to come from existing householders and little action was initially taken. Up to this time rented housing had been provided by private landlords or large industrial concerns like the Fife Coal Company. The First World War, with its aspiration for men to come back to 'Homes Fit for Heroes', gave added impetus to the need for better houses and in 1917 a Royal Commission reported on the dreadful state of housing in industrial communities. It urged local authorities to become involved, even though they had little or no experience in the field. After the war councils everywhere embarked on projects to provide public housing and through the 1920s and 30s built numerous schemes like the one in Kelty, which had Centre Street at its heart and included Oak Street, seen here. There was clearly an attempt to give these houses a distinctive appearance with the varied use of harling and bricks.

The Second World War interrupted the construction of council houses, but as soon as the conflict was over Fife County Council began building in Kelty on the sloping ground west of Blair Street. This scheme was different from the old Kelty because it was based on proper town planning, and instead of straight roads included streets with curving lines and open urban spaces like Blackhall Square. It acted as link with the older scheme through Centre Street, which is seen in the centre of this picture. The new scheme was also the location of additional shops including Keltyhill post office and a branch of the Kelty Co-operative Society, which can just be seen on the left. This was opened in 1951 and is thought to have been Fife's first self-service store. Curious retailers came from a wide area to inspect this newfangled idea, but the march of the supermarkets eventually proved too much for this little pioneer, which closed in 1990.

Despite the provision of shops like the co-op, vans such as the one on the right of this picture of Keltyhill Crescent still toured the streets selling produce. The new scheme included a variety of house types. Some of them were made of steel and concrete, others were of brick and there were a few Swedish timber houses and aluminium prefabs. The development was planned to contain 600 houses in total, and by the middle of 1948, when Keltyhill Crescent was occupied, 200 had been completed and another 200 were under construction. At that time the coal industry had just been nationalised, Lanarkshire's old pits were being closed and Fife was seen as the principal development area in Scotland. Mining families from the west were being encouraged to move east and they needed houses, as did local people moving from old substandard accommodation.

A cryptic note on the back of this postcard reads 'April '68' and describes the view as 'looking south'. It could equally have noted that it shows the west side of Main Street, which is where all of Kelty's early houses were situated, strung out along the one side of the road for a considerable distance, creating a big problem for water supply and drainage. The two-storeyed housing development on the right, at the corner of Croall Place, replaced some older single-storey buildings not long before this picture was taken. The Gothenburg Hall, with its clock tower, can be seen in the far distance while in the centre of the picture is the Crown Inn. It was built on this site in 1904, possibly superseding an earlier pub in Croall Place. There were a number of licensed premises in Kelty before and after the Goths were set up, providing competition and ensuring that the coal company didn't control everything that happened in the village. Out of sight on the left are Kelty's schools and the Moray Institute.

The Earl of Moray left money in his will for various projects, including a library and institute for Kelty. This was not the first library in the village, as one had been set up in 1890 in a room made available by the Fife Coal Company and furnished with books purchased using a grant of £39 from the Andrew Carnegie Trust. Ten years later the Countess of Moray opened the new Library and Moray Institute. In 1922 the newly established Miners' Welfare Fund paid for improvements, and five years later financed a major reconstruction scheme which effectively made the facility into a Miners' Institute. Across Bath Street, on the site now occupied by the health centre, was the Aitken Baths, seen here on the right. These were named after Thomas Aitken of Nivingston, chairman of the Fife Coal Company, who gifted them to the people of Kelty. They were opened in June 1901 and comprised a 30 foot by 20 foot swimming 'pond' with suspended rings, plus Russian Baths, sprays and a slipper bath. The complex was destroyed by fire in 1925 and not rebuilt despite attempts to finance this using the Miners' Welfare Fund. The primary school in the background was built to the designs of John Houston between 1895 and 1897, although the date on the facade is 1896.

Beath School Board was set up following the Education Act of 1872 and a few years later erected a four-roomed school in Kelty. More buildings were put up around it as the school population grew. Some are still in use although the one seen in the centre of this picture was burned down in 1983. To its right is the school house and on the left the Free Church. There had been a Free Church congregation in Beath Parish since 1843 when, in an event known as the Disruption, the Church of Scotland split over the issue of who had the right to choose a minister, the congregation or a powerful patron. A small Free Church was set up at the north end of the village in what became known as Church Row (Kirk Raw), but Kelty's rapid growth in the late nineteenth century demanded a larger place of worship, and this replacement building was designed by T. Hyslop Ure and erected in 1895/96. When the Free and United Presbyterian Churches came together in 1900 it became the Moray United Free Church, and following the amalgamation of Kelty's two United Free Church congregations in 1929 it was renamed the North Church. After 1974, when the congregation joined that of the Church of Scotland, the vacated North Church building was taken over as a community education centre, later becoming Kelty Community Centre.

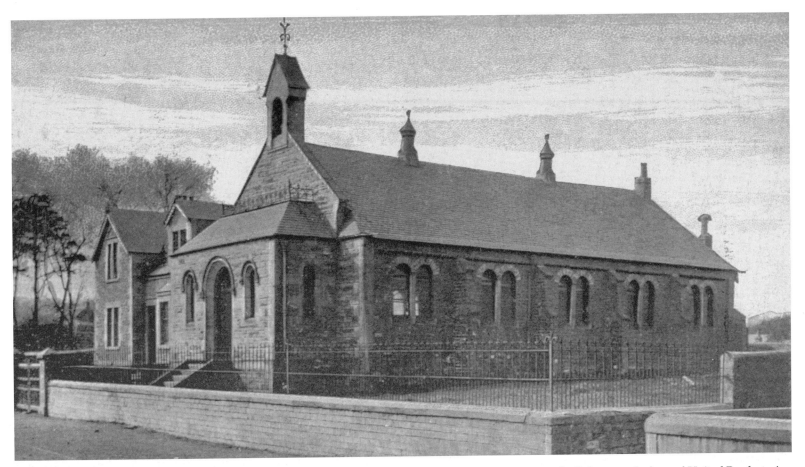

Kelty's third Protestant church was in fact the first of the trio dating from the 1890s to be completed. It was built for a newly formed United Presbyterian congregation and opened at the end of January 1896. Designed by an Alloa architectural firm, it was made of brick with a stone frontage and could accommodate 350 worshipers. The site in Mossgreen Street was donated to the church on condition that, although it only took up half of it, it paid the feu for the whole area. The United Presbyterian Church had its origins in an early split from the Established Church over the right of congregations to choose their own ministers. Known as the Secession Church, it was constituted in 1733 in a ceremony at Gairney Bridge, about three miles north of Kelty. Over a period of 100 years the Secession Church itself split into various factions before coming together again in 1847 as the United Presbyterian Church. When this amalgamated with the Free Church in 1900 the little church became known as Trinity United Free, and became a church hall when Kelty's Free Church congregations combined in 1929.

Kelty had both instrumental and pipe bands. The instrumental band came first and apparently owes its origins to four young men who, in the early 1850s, went around the farms and big houses collecting money for instruments. This early picture suggests that those initial funds didn't stretch to buying uniforms, although by the start of the twentieth century the band was fully kitted out and employing a professional conductor. Funding was also put on a more secure basis with regular donations being deducted from miners' pay packets, a practice that was common throughout the coal industry. After the First World War the band also had a hall it could call its own – a wooden hut purchased as government surplus and re-erected near the foot of Keltyhill Road. This was shared with the pipe band, which appears to have been formed almost 50 years after the instrumental band. Both bands were known by the name Kelty & Blairadam and achieved significant success in their respective competitions.

The Kelty Musical Association ensured that the two bands were not the only music-makers to bring fame to the village. Formed in 1932, the association became noted for its musicals and light operas. Shows were initially staged in the Gothenburg Hall, but these were confined to midweek nights so that the auditorium could still be used to screen movies at the weekends. This arrangement continued through the 1930s and for the first production staged after the Second World War, *The Desert Song*, some of the cast of which are seen here. Thereafter the association put its productions on at the Carnegie Hall in Dunfermline. This exposure to a wider public helped it to attract larger audiences and become one of the most popular amateur light opera groups in the country. The staging of *Oklahoma* in 1955 was a particular success, running for three weeks including Saturday matinees.

The north end of Main Street seen in the 1960s looking down Stewart's Brae, with the tenements known as Stewart's Buildings on the right. Dating from c.1900, these appear to have been built with expansion in mind, but since nothing else went up alongside them they remained out of scale with their surroundings. The hoarding alongside is displaying an advertisement for cigarettes that would be illegal today. In the distance, facing up the brae, is the building erected as No. 4 Goth, with No. 3 Goth halfway up the street on the left. This is now the Lindsay Tavern, previously called Blairadam Tavern and the Three Swans of Blairadam. On the north gable of this building is a stair which led to an upper floor segregated from the drinking part of the establishment on the ground floor. This allowed people to attend teetotal functions without having to be exposed to the sight, smell and sound of drink being taken. The out-of-scale tenements have now been replaced by the Community Garden, and few other buildings seen here remain.

The houses in the centre of this picture of Kelty's north end are known as Whitegates Cottages, a name derived from the railway level crossing gates that can just be discerned between the first pair of houses and the next ones down the hill. The crossing was removed long ago, but Whitegates Terrace keeps the old name alive. The mineral line associated with the gates ran past the village gasworks and on up to Blairenbathie Colliery. It was noted for having a 1 in 30 gradient and crossing the valley of the Kelty Burn on a high brick and wood structure known as the '100 foot bridge'. The old trackbed is now a walkway incorporating a bridge taking it over the motorway. On the right are the houses of Black Street with the familiar shape of Benarty rising above them.

North End and Benarty Hill, Kelty.

Tucked in behind Whitegates Cottages and the building with the dormer windows in the upper picture was Earl's Row, a small terrace of miners' houses built in 1914 by the Fife Coal Company. It consisted of eight two-apartment houses with sculleries and toilets. It has now been replaced by a new Earl's Row.

39

People have become used to natural gas being piped from sources many miles away, but 100 years ago gas had to be generated in an industrial process. Coal, the basic raw material, was baked in retorts at temperatures of 1,000 °C to extract the gas, which was then purified, washed and stored in large gas holders ready for use. The spent coal from which the gas had been extracted was known as coke and sold as a usable fuel. There were gasworks in many towns, but Kelty would not have been one of them if proposals put forward by the Cowdenbeath Gas Company in 1904 to supply the village had been accepted. Instead the Kelty Co-operative Society and the Fife Coal Company jointly set up a gasworks on the site of the old Kelty No. 1 Pit and adjacent brickworks. Gas was also piped from the works to Lochore. Kelty could even boast a gas showroom plus housing for the company's employees, some of whom are seen here beside the works.

Following its acquisition of the large Cowdenbeath Coal Company in 1896, the Fife Coal Company set about buying up all the small pits around Kelty, including Blairadam Colliery and Brickworks in 1902. Brick-making plants were often set up in coal-mining areas because the minerals used in the process were found together: clays were formed from the mud at the bottom of the lake or swamp where the trees that formed coal grew millions of years ago. It helped as well to have a ready source of fuel to fire the ovens. Blairadam Colliery closed on the last day of 1924, but output at the brickworks was expanded the following year and this growth continued through the war years. Decline and closure coincided with the demise of the coal industry, and the site of the abandoned works, and adjacent blaes quarry, became a derelict eyesore. With financial help from the Scottish Development Agency it was cleared and landscaped over the course of two years, and opened as Blairadam Park in 1981.

The hill known as Benarty is a distinctive feature to the north of Kelty, like an old and constant friend in a changing world. In their leisure time miners liked to head for the slopes where they would sit, drink beer, soak up the fresh air and enjoy the wide skies and panoramic views of the surrounding countryside. Picnics on the hill with wives and children were popular too. This picture, probably taken from the back of the Fife Coal Company's brick-built Grievesland Terrace houses at the foot of Main Street, shows a scene that would be almost unrecognisable today without Benarty in the background. The houses to the right are still there, although much altered, but the rest of Black Road has been built up around them. Also, the practice of having a huge washing day, with access to communal laundry facilities allocated to different tenants in rotation, has died out and the sight of so many sheets and clothes billowing in the wind is now rare.

The washing day ritual was just one of many activities that were somehow typical of domestic life in any mining community. Some others are evident in this evocative picture, thought to show a family in Mossgreen Street. Behind the woman and the little girls is a shed for homing pigeons – fleein' doos (flying pigeons) was one of the most popular of miners' pastimes. Racing dugs (dogs) was another passion, as was tending the garden, or if that was small or non-existent tending the allotment instead, and there were many of these around Kelty. Growing vegetables not only gave men the chance to be out in the healthy open air, but also provided good, cheap produce for the kitchen. So did the practice of keeping chickens which supplied the family with fresh eggs and, when the hens stopped laying, they too went into the pot and tasted a lot better than the pumped-up, battery-reared supermarket products available today.

One of Kelty's greatest claims to fame is as the home of one-time world draughts champion, Bob Stewart. He lived at Keltybridge, in the cottage on the left of this picture which is now graced with a porch at the front door. These days chess has gained a higher public profile and draughts seems to have fallen out of fashion, but in Bob Stewart's time it was popular and highly competitive, with leagues operating at various levels. He won the first of five successive Scottish championships at the age of nineteen and gave up competing for the title in his early twenties after winning three times without losing a game. Nevertheless he continued to play at international level for Scotland and in various tournaments, including at least one in America. He gave exhibition games playing simultaneous matches and, in an exceptional feat of memory, also played matches blindfold. In 1922 he contested the world championship with American Newell Banks. The match was held in Glasgow and the result was in doubt up to the last of 40 games, with Bob Stewart taking the title with two wins, one loss and 37 draws. He remained undefeated for the next fifteen years and retired on medical advice in 1937, dying in 1941.

The border between Fife and Kinross-shire is formed by the Kelty Burn, so the community of Keltybridge is split between the two areas. Originally it was known as Bridgend and was all on the Kinross side. It was home to miners who worked on coal outcrops exposed by the burn as its course cut down through the strata. The bridge over the Kelty Burn is thought to have been built in the mid-eighteenth century, although there is also a carved stone let into the west side of the structure which is dated 1696. At some time the wall leading into the bridge on the left has been straightened and is no longer kinked as seen here. Half-hidden by trees on the right is a building that was used for a time as a post office and sweetie shop. Modernisation has resulted in a few inevitable changes, and although the house on the left has gone this attractive little village remains largely unspoiled. The houses sitting with their gable ends to the road, rather than facing it, add to the appeal.

William Adam, perhaps the most prominent architect of his day, bought the estate of Blair Crambeth, to the north of Kelty, in 1733 and changed its name to Blairadam. He and his sons John and Robert, who also became architects, were so successful and made the Adam name so famous that the style they created is still looked on as one of the great movements in the history of building and interior decoration. Their work on buildings such as Pollok House in Glasgow, Culzean Castle in Ayrshire and Charlotte Square in Edinburgh is so fine it makes the contrast with the family home all the more remarkable, because Blairadam itself is just an ordinary Scots house lacking any obvious style or adornment. As is often the way with country houses, it was added to over the years by successive generations of the family, with perhaps the only obvious Adam feature in this view being the pedimented porch attributed to John Adam.

The Kinross-shire Railway was one of many small companies set up in the mid-nineteenth century to lay sections of track. Its line between Kinross and Cowdenbeath was completed by 1860 and connected with the tracks of other companies at both ends. It was all a bit haphazard, but in the 1860s many of these small concerns were quickly swallowed up by larger operators, and the Kinross-shire became part of the giant North British Railway (NBR) which gained a near monopoly of railways in Fife. On its board was one William Patrick Adam of Blairadam who had become MP for Kinross and Clackmannan in 1859. He may have had some influence over the siting of this station at Blairadam. When the NBR built the Forth Bridge in 1890 and made the line a major through-route between Edinburgh and Perth, the size and frequency of trains increased, but neither Kelty nor Blairadam Stations derived long-term benefit, possibly because of the distance people had to walk to get to them. Both were closed in September 1930.

The nearby Blairadam Estate was a big attraction for Kelty folk. It was a place of peace and pleasure for the children who went there on Sunday school picnics, and also for the golfers who used it for a decade or so prior to the Second World War. Others, however, stole into the woods, drawn by the irresistible lure of poachable game. Some got caught (trapping rabbits!), but no doubt many a Kelty pot sang to the tune of free food from the outdoor larder on their doorstep. The tangle of Blairadam Woods and Benarty's rough terrain also left their mark on the author as an orienteer in his younger days!

At Maryburgh, Kelty

AT MARYBURGH KELTY.

In order to improve their estate the Adams needed other sources of income than the money they earned designing buildings, and indeed much of the wealth which they generated came from coal. The family was fortunate in having seams that outcropped on the estate allowing relatively easy exploitation. The miners who came to dig the coal, however, needed somewhere to live and the now picturesque village of Maryburgh was developed about 1740 to provide them with housing.